Dominoes

Sherlock Holmes:

The Emerald Crown

OXFORD

UNIVERSITY PRESS

OXFORD
UNIVERSITY PRESS

Great Clarendon Street, Oxford OX2 6DP

Oxford University Press is a department of the University of Oxford.
It furthers the University's objective of excellence in research, scholarship,
and education by publishing worldwide in

Oxford New York

Auckland Cape Town Dar es Salaam Hong Kong Karachi
Kuala Lumpur Madrid Melbourne Mexico City Nairobi
New Delhi Shanghai Taipei Toronto

With offices in

Argentina Austria Brazil Chile Czech Republic France Greece
Guatemala Hungary Italy Japan Poland Portugal Singapore
South Korea Switzerland Thailand Turkey Ukraine Vietnam

OXFORD and OXFORD ENGLISH are registered trade marks of
Oxford University Press in the UK and in certain other countries

ISBN: 978 0 19 424452 7

A complete audio recording of this Dominoes edition of
Sherlock Holmes: The Emerald Crown is available

Printed in Hong Kong

ACKNOWLEDGEMENTS

Cover illustration by: Susan Scott
Main Text Illustrations by: Marcela Hajdinjak-Krec pp 1, 4, 6, 7, 8, 9, 10, 11, 13, 15, 17,
18, 19, 22, 24, 26, 29, 31, 32, 35, 37, 38, 39, 43

*The publisher would like to thank the following for their kind permission to reproduce photos
and other copyright material*: Alamy pp 41 (Crown/Peter Bonek, St Stephen's Crown/Peter
Barritt, The Pahlavi Crown/Popperfoto); Britain on View pp 40 (Tower of London/Britain
on View); Getty Images pp 41 (Fabergé Egg/Laski Diffusion/East News/Laison); TopFoto
pp 41 (Imperial Crown Jewels/Topham/Woodmanstern)

Dominoes

SERIES EDITORS: BILL BOWLER AND SUE PARMINTER

Sherlock Holmes:
The Emerald Crown

SIR ARTHUR CONAN DOYLE

Text adaptation by Janet Hardy-Gould

Illustrated by Marcela Hajdinjak-Krec

LEVEL ONE ■ 400 HEADWORDS

Sir Arthur Conan Doyle (1859-1930), born in Edinburgh, Scotland, is best known as the creator of Sherlock Holmes. He started writing after working as a doctor and soon became one of the world's best-known authors. Four other books by Conan Doyle are also available as Dominoes: three Sherlock Holmes stories, *The Blue Diamond*, *The Norwood Mystery* and *The Sign of Four*, and an adventure story, *The Lost World*.

OXFORD
UNIVERSITY PRESS

BEFORE READING

1 **Here are some of the people in *The Emerald Crown*. Who takes the crown?**

a Alexander Holder, a banker

b Arthur Holder, Mr Holder's son

c Sir George Burnwell, Arthur Holder's friend

d Mary Holder, Mr Holder's niece

e Lucy, Mr Holder's maid

f Francis Prosper, Lucy's friend

2 **What does the criminal do with the crown?**

The criminal …

a ☐ takes the crown to a different country.

b ☐ breaks the crown and takes some of the emeralds from it.

c ☐ sells the crown for a lot of money.

d ☐ hides the crown in a tree for many years.

3 **What do you think happens at the end of the story?**

～ Chapter one ～
A strange man

'**H**olmes,' I said one morning. 'Come over here to the window. There's a very **strange** man in our street.'

My friend, the famous detective Sherlock Holmes, got up slowly from his chair. He stood behind me, with his hands in his pockets, and looked down into Baker Street. It was a cold February morning, and the **snow** of the day before was on the road.

The man in the street was about fifty, tall, and fat. He wore expensive clothes – a long black coat, a tall hat and dark trousers. He ran along the street, and he looked very **worried**. His hands went up and down quickly, and his head moved from left to right.

'*There's a very strange man in our street.*'

Holmes /hɔʊmz/

strange not usual

snow something soft, cold, and white

worried not happy about something and thinking a lot about it

1

'What's wrong with him?' I said. 'He's looking at the numbers on all the houses.'

'Watson,' said Holmes. 'He's coming here, I think.'

'Here?' I asked.

'Yes,' said Holmes. 'He's very unhappy about something, and he wants my help.'

Just then, the man stopped at our front door.

'There . . . I told you, Watson,' said Holmes with a smile. 'He's here to see me.'

Not long after that, the **maid** brought the man up to our room. Soon he stood in front of us. His head moved from left to right, and he put his hand up worriedly and **pulled** his hair from time to time. His mouth opened, but he couldn't speak.

Holmes took him by the arm and smiled. 'Please sit down,' he said, and he took him across the room to one of the chairs, and sat down next to him. 'You'd like to tell us your story. Is that right? You are tired. We can wait a minute, and when you are ready, we can begin.'

The man sat for a minute or two. Holmes and I waited quietly. Then, when he was ready, the man looked up and began. 'I look very strange, I know,' he said quietly.

'No, no,' said Holmes. 'You want to tell me something important, that's all.'

'Why did this happen to me? It's the worst thing . . . the very worst,' said the stranger.

'Please tell me your name, sir, and then you can tell me your story,' said Holmes.

'Perhaps you know my name,' said our visitor slowly. 'I am Alexander Holder of the Holder and Stevenson **Bank** of Threadneedle Street.'

maid a woman who works in a rich person's house

pull to move something strongly towards you

bank people put money and expensive things here

2

'Ah yes,' said Holmes. 'One of the oldest banks in London.'

'I'm sorry, sir,' said Holder. 'They told me about you and said, "You must speak to Sherlock Holmes. He can help you!" I came to see you at once. I ran from Baker Street **station** to get here more quickly. It looked strange, I know, because I don't usually go running. Thank you for waiting. I am ready now to begin.'

Holder then started to tell us his story:

Yesterday morning I was in my office at the bank when a man came to see me. When I saw him, I was very **surprised**. He was a very famous man. I'm sorry, but I can't tell you his name – because he's one of the British **royal family.**

'Mr Holder,' he said, 'people come to you to **borrow** money, I hear.'

'Yes, they do,' I said, 'and we always give it to them when we can.'

'I see,' said the man. 'Well, I need to borrow fifty thousand pounds from you at once.'

'Fifty thousand?' I said.

'Yes. I can borrow that money many times over from my friends, of course. But I wanted to come to a bank for it. It's not good to borrow from friends. After you give the money back to them, they always ask you for things later to say "thank you".'

'And how long do you need this money?' I asked.

'For six days,' said the man. 'Someone is going to give me a lot of money on Monday, so I can give back the fifty thousand pounds to you then. But I need the money now.'

'Well, for the bank to give out fifty thousand pounds, you need to leave something expensive with us,' I said.

station people get on and off trains here

surprised feeling that something very new is suddenly happening

royal family the family of the king or queen

borrow to take for a short time

3

The man then took out a big black box and put it on the table. I was very surprised when he opened it.

'Do you know the **Emerald Crown**?' he said.

'It's one of the most famous crowns in England,' I answered.

Well, this man took the Emerald Crown out of the box. It's **gold** with thirty-nine large emeralds – all of the most beautiful green colour.

'Do you know the Emerald Crown?'

emerald a very expensive green stone

crown a king wears this on his head

gold an expensive yellow metal

4

He told me, 'Please be very careful with it, and don't take it away from the bank.'

He also said, 'Please don't tell any of your friends or family about it.'

He was afraid of a **scandal** for the royal family, I think.

Well, I gave the man the fifty thousand pounds. He thanked me, and quickly left the bank. He's going to come back on Monday morning for the crown.

But then I started to feel worried. One night last week somebody went into a bank not far from us in Threadneedle Street, and took a hundred thousand pounds from the building. I was unhappy about leaving the Emerald Crown at the bank. So last night I took it home with me.

I left work at about six o'clock. I closed the door of the bank behind me and I looked carefully up and down Threadneedle Street. In the dark nobody saw me put the black box under my coat. I then took a **carriage** back to my house in **Streatham**. It was, of course, a cold, snowy evening and the carriage drove along very slowly. There was only one man in the carriage with me and he didn't see the box, I know: I had it under my coat all the time.

I felt pleased when I arrived home. I ran upstairs to my office and put the black box into the **desk** there. I **locked** the desk with a **key** and then went over to the window. Just then, I saw somebody – a stranger – in the front garden.

I couldn't see his face. He wore a hat and a long coat. When he saw me at the window, he suddenly walked away. I remember one thing about him: when he walked, one of his legs moved strangely.

I then ran quickly downstairs and out into the garden. 'Hello. Who's there?' I called.

scandal something that a lot of people talk about, in an angry or interested way

carriage an old kind of car that horses pull

Streatham /ˈstretəm /

desk a table in a study or in an office

lock to close with a key

key you can open or close a lock with this

READING CHECK

Are these sentences true or false? Tick the boxes.

		True	False
a	It was a cold day in February, with snow on the road.	✓	☐
b	Mr Holder looked worried when he spoke to Holmes.	☐	☐
c	The Holder and Stevenson Bank is one of the newest London banks.	☐	☐
d	A man from the Spanish royal family came to the bank.	☐	☐
e	The man was afraid of a scandal.	☐	☐
f	The man borrowed five hundred pounds from Holder.	☐	☐
g	Holder took the Emerald Crown to his house.	☐	☐
h	Holder saw a strange woman in the front garden.	☐	☐

WORD WORK

1 Match the words with the pictures.

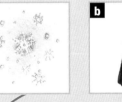

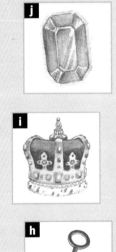

1 desk	**6** carriage
2 emerald	**7** surprised
3 crown	**8** key
4 maid	**9** gold
5 snow	**10** lock

2 Use the words from Activity 1 to complete these sentences.

a It was a cold day, and there was a lot of .....snow..... on the road.

b The royal family had a big .... with six white horses.

c When they arrived at the house, the .... answered the door.

d When you leave, please .... the front door with this big ....

e She needed a pen and some paper, so she looked in the .... for them.

f Anastasia wore a beautiful .... on her head. It had a big green .... at the front.

g He bought an expensive .... watch for his wife last Christmas.

h She looked very .... when we suddenly arrived at her house.

GUESS WHAT

What does Alexander Holder do in the next chapter? Read the sentences and write *Yes* or *No*.

Holder ...

a talks to the strange man in the garden. ......

b hits the strange man. ......

c talks to the people in his family about the Emerald Crown. ......

d runs away with the Emerald Crown. ......

Chapter TWO

Holder's story

continue to start again after stopping

wild excited; not doing what someone wants

gambling club a place where you can play games and win money

play cards to play a game (like poker) with a pack of cards

'And did you find this man in the long coat and hat?' I asked.

'No,' answered Holder. 'I looked in the front and back garden, but nobody was there.'

He stopped talking, and thought for a minute. 'But before I **continue** with my story, I must tell you about my family, and all the different people in the house.'

'Ah yes,' said Holmes, and he moved his chair nearer.

'My family isn't very big,' said Holder. 'My wife died ten years ago and I've got only one son, Arthur. I'm sorry to say it, but he isn't a very good son.

'When my wife died, Arthur was the most important thing for me. I wanted to make him happy, so when he asked for something, I gave it to him. I was wrong to do it. I know that now.

'I wanted Arthur to work with me at the bank, but he was no good with money. He was a **wild** young man. When he was eighteen, he started going to a **gambling club**. He made friends there – all rich young men with a lot of time and money. With these new friends he learned to **play cards** but, of course, he often lost. He came to me nearly every week and asked, "Can I borrow some more money from you father?"'

'*He was a wild young man.*'

8

'And did you give it to him?' I asked interestedly.

'Yes,' said Holder. 'Arthur often told me, "Father, I'm going to leave the club!" And from time to time he stopped going there. But he always went back after a week or two. There was one friend at the club with a lot of **power** over Arthur, an older man – Burnwell.'

Burnwell

'Burnwell?' asked Holmes.

'Yes, Sir George Burnwell. Do you know him?'

'I know his name, I think,' said Holmes. He looked quickly over at me.

'When Burnwell first came to our house, I liked him,' continued Holder. 'He's a tall, **handsome** man. When he walks into a room, everybody looks at him. He's a wonderful talker: he can tell the most interesting stories for hours and hours.

power being able to make somebody or something do what you want

handsome good-looking

niece your sister's (or brother's) daughter

'But he has a cold look in his eyes,' said Holder slowly. 'For me there's something strange about him. And my Mary thinks this, too. I can see it in her eyes.'

'Who's Mary?' I asked.

'Mary is my **niece**,' said Holder. 'When my brother died five years ago, she came to live with us.

Mary

'Lucy, our most important maid.'

'She's a wonderful girl,' continued Holder, 'and she does everything for me at home. I call her my "right hand", you know.' Holder looked out of the window and smiled. But the smile suddenly left his face.

'Only one thing makes me unhappy,' said Holder. 'Arthur loves Mary very much. Last year, he asked Mary to **marry** him, but she said "no". I feel very sorry about this, because Arthur needs a good wife. And Mary is the most wonderful girl.'

Holder stopped talking and then, after a minute or two, began again. 'Now, where was I?' he asked. 'Ah, yes . . . yes. Of course, there are the maids in the house too. There are three of them – good young girls, and all of them started with me a number of years ago. And then there's Lucy, our most important maid. She came to us two months ago. We're very happy with her. But the only thing is . . .'

'What's that?' I asked.

'She's very beautiful, and she has many **admirers**. Sometimes they come to the **kitchen** door in the evening . . .' Holder then stopped. 'Well, that's everybody at home, I think.'

'And what about yesterday evening?' asked Holmes.

'Oh, yes, my story,' said Holder. 'When I came back into the house, it was time for dinner. And after dinner, Lucy brought in some coffee for Arthur, Mary, and me. Over coffee, I told Arthur and Mary all about the Emerald

marry to make someone your wife or husband

admirer an old word for a person who likes or loves another person, often secretly

kitchen the room in the house where people make things to eat

Crown. Lucy was out of the room at this time, I think, but I'm not **sure**.

'Arthur and Mary were very surprised when I said, "The famous crown is upstairs in my desk." Of course, they wanted to see it but I said "no". Arthur was very worried about house **thieves**. But I told him, "Everything's all right because there's a good lock on the desk." But he laughed and said, "Any key opens that desk. I opened it with the key to the **attic** when I was a child."

'I didn't listen much to Arthur,' said Holder. 'He often talks wildly about things. And by this time I was tired, so I went upstairs to bed.

'After about ten minutes, Arthur came to my room. He asked, "Can I borrow some money, father? I need two hundred pounds this time – to give back to my friends at the gambling club!" I felt very angry: he wanted money for the second time in a week. When I said "no", he started to cry. He then walked slowly to the door and closed it angrily behind him.'

'When I said "no" he started to cry.'

READING CHECK

Match the two parts of these sentences.

a	Alexander Holder…	**1**	has a lot of power over Arthur.
b	Alexander Holder's wife…	**2**	come to the kitchen door.
c	Arthur Holder…	**3**	tells Arthur and Mary about the crown.
d	Mary…	**4**	is dead.
e	Sir George Burnwell…	**5**	doesn't want to marry Arthur.
f	Arthur's friends at the gambling club…	**6**	is very beautiful.
g	Lucy the maid…	**7**	often wants to borrow money.
h	Lucy's admirers…	**8**	have a lot of time and money.

WORD WORK

1 Find ten more words from Chapter 1 in the wordsquare.

```
Q C O N T I N U E V S
P L A Y C A R D S T L
O B S L M A R R Y W G
W R U F E B X O N I T
E Y R Y P M A H I L G
R W E C Y G T S E D R
T H I E F J T Q C V L
V Z X A D M I R E R S
N F W K T U C Y M G E
H A N D S O M E F X E
```

2 Use the words from Activity 1 to complete the dialogues.

a 'Shall I stop playing the guitar now?'

'No. Please ..continue..'

b 'Where's your room?'

'It's upstairs in the ....'

c 'Who's that little girl over there with your brother?'

'That's my ....'

d 'Would you like to .... with us?'

'I'm not .... I haven't got a lot of time.'

e 'Emily, that boy can't stop looking at Victoria. Does your sister have an ....?'

'Yes, she does, Charlotte. His name's Albert. He's very ...., I think.'

f 'Look! A .... is taking that woman's bag.'

'Quick, phone the police.'

g 'That film star is going to .... his girlfriend next week.'

'It can't be true. He's a really .... young man and he goes out with a different woman every night!'

h 'Would you like to be rich?'

'Yes, of course. Money gives you ....'

GUESS WHAT

In the next chapter Alexander Holder gets up when he hears a noise in the night. What is it? Tick one box.

a ☐ A woman is crying downstairs.

b ☐ Somebody is breaking a window.

c ☐ Somebody is closing a door or a window.

d ☐ Two people are talking in the garden.

Chapter THREE

In the night

Holmes sat back in his chair. 'Well, Mr Holder, what happened next?' he asked. Holder continued with his story.

Before I got into bed last night, I looked into all the different rooms in the house. I went first to the office next to my room. I looked into the desk. The Emerald Crown was there, and it was **safe**. I then locked the desk again carefully.

After that I went downstairs. I was surprised when I found Mary next to an open window in the **hall**. She quickly closed the window when she saw me.

'**Uncle**,' she said. 'Five minutes ago Lucy came in through the kitchen door. She was out in the **lane**. Did you know that?'

'No, I did not,' I said angrily.

'She was with one of her admirers again, I think,' said Mary. 'It isn't safe. We don't want strange men near the house at night.'

'No, we don't. I must talk to her in the morning about this. And Mary,' I said. 'Did you lock all the doors?'

'Yes, I did,' she said.

'Are you sure?'

'Yes, I'm sure.'

Then I went upstairs to bed. I'm not usually a good sleeper and sometimes I get up in the night. Well, at about 2 o'clock in the morning I suddenly opened my eyes when I heard a strange noise.

It wasn't a **loud** noise. 'Is someone closing a window or a door perhaps?' I thought. I sat up in bed and listened.

Everything was quiet for a minute or two, but then I heard somebody in my office. I felt afraid and got out of bed. I went to

safe in no danger

hall a room in the middle of the house from which you can go to all the other rooms

uncle the brother of your father (or mother)

lane a narrow road

loud making a lot of noise; not quiet

'Arthur!
You thief!
You thief!'

the office, and slowly opened the door.

In the half-light I could see Arthur in only his shirt and trousers. He had no shoes on. The Emerald Crown was in his hands, and he pulled at it wildly. He wanted to break it, I think.

'Arthur!' I cried. 'What are you doing with the crown? You thief! You thief!'

When he heard me, the colour left his face, and the crown **fell** from his hands.

I ran over and looked at it. One of the **corners** of the crown, with three emeralds on it, was missing.

'Arthur!' I said. 'Where are the **missing** emeralds?'

'The emeralds?' he asked quietly.

'Yes,' I said. 'The emeralds.'

'But surely they are all here,' he answered.

'Look, there are three emeralds missing. Do I need to call you a **liar** and a thief?' I cried.

fall (*past* **fell**) to go down suddenly

corner where the two sides of something meet

missing not there

liar a person who says things that are not true

15

'Liar? Thief?' said Arthur angrily. 'I'm not going to listen to your names.'

'But I saw you with the crown in your hands,' I said. 'You wanted to break it!'

'You're wrong! You don't understand!' said Arthur 'I—' He then stopped suddenly, and said. 'I'm not going to say one more word about any of this. I'm going to leave the house in the morning, and never come back!'

'You're going to leave this house in the hands of the **police**,' I cried.

'Call the police then,' said Arthur. 'It doesn't matter to me.'

By this time everybody in the house was out of bed. Mary ran into the room. When she saw the crown and Arthur's face, she understood everything. With a cry, she fell suddenly into a chair.

I called for one of the maids and told her, 'Get the police!' When two police officers arrived at the door, Arthur looked white and ill. He stood with his head down. 'Are you **really** going to give me to the police, father?' he asked.

'Yes,' I answered. 'You know the crown is the royal family's. The police need to **investigate** this **crime** carefully. We must find the missing emeralds or there's going to be a scandal in this country.'

Arthur listened and then looked up at me. 'Can I ask for one thing, father? Can I leave the house for five minutes?'

'Leave the house for five minutes!' I said. 'Leave you free to run away or put the missing emeralds somewhere safe? No! No, of course you can't.'

I then started to talk quietly. 'Please, Arthur. I'm a famous banker. I have a lot to lose here. Give me back the emeralds now, and we can forget everything.'

'And forget your names for me – "liar" and "thief"? Never!'

police they find people who do something bad

really truly

investigate to find out about something

crime killing someone or taking something from someone

16

cried Arthur, and his face was red and angry.

There was nothing more to say. I called the police officers into the room and gave Arthur to them. 'Look over the house upstairs and downstairs!' I said. 'Go into every room. Only stop looking when you find the missing emeralds!'

The police were in the house for hours, but they found nothing. And Arthur? He didn't open his mouth again. He didn't say a word. He sat there with his head in his hands.

Early this morning, the police took Arthur away. I went with him, and then talked to the head officer at the police station. He couldn't understand the **case**. He gave me your name and address, and so I came quickly here to Baker Street.

case when the police work to find answers

I badly need your help, Mr Holmes. Last night, I lost everything: the emeralds, my son, and my good name. You must help me to get them back.

Early this morning, the police took Arthur away.

READING CHECK

Put these sentences in the correct order. Number them 1–8.

a ☐ Two police officers arrive at the house.

b ☐ Holder hears a noise at two o'clock in the morning.

c ☐ Mary comes into the office. She falls suddenly into a chair.

d ☐ Holder looks into the desk. The crown is safe.

e ☐ Arthur wants to leave the house for five minutes.

f ☐ Holder sees Mary next to an open window.

g ☐ The police take Arthur away.

h ☐ Holder sees Arthur with the crown. The corner is missing.

WORD WORK

Find words in the emeralds to complete the sentences.

a That's my u n c l e Mark. He's my mother's brother. *neuel*

b I can't do my homework because your radio is very l _ _ _. *doul*

c Your bag isn't in the kitchen, perhaps it's in the h _ _ _. *lhal*

d Oh, no, I can't find my watch. It's m _ _ _ _ _ _ again. *imsisgn*

e There was an accident today. The police are going to i _ _ _ _ _ _ _ _ _ _ it. *venis gteait*

f Do you think he r _ _ _ _ _ loves her or is he only interested in her money? *ealryl*

g His story isn't true. He's a l _ _ _. *rlai*

h We heard about the c _ _ _ _ on the radio. The thief took a million dollars. *rmice*

i It's a very strange c _-_ _ and the police don't understand it. *asce*

GUESS WHAT

In the next chapter Holmes goes to Holder's house. What does he do? Tick the boxes.

a Holmes walks for a long time in the . . .

1 ☐ garden.   **2** ☐ attic.

b Holmes asks . . . a lot of questions.

1 ☐ Lucy.   **2** ☐ Mary.

c Holmes looks carefully at the . . .

1 ☐ hall window.   **2** ☐ front door.

Chapter FOUR

The house in Streatham

Holder sat and closed his eyes. He moved in his chair unhappily. Holmes looked out of the window into Baker Street. I waited for him to speak about this most interesting case.

'Do you have a lot of visitors?' Holmes asked Holder suddenly.

'Not many,' said Holder. 'Stevenson, from the bank comes to the house sometimes. And there's Arthur's friend, Sir George Burnwell.'

'And do you go out often?' asked Holmes.

'Arthur does,' said Holder. 'But Mary and I stay at home.'

'And is Mary worried about the case?' asked Holmes.

'Yes,' said Holder. 'She didn't sleep at all last night.'

Holmes moved nearer to Holder. 'But is your son really **guilty**? How can you be sure of it?' he asked.

'I saw him with the crown in his hands!' said Holder.

'That looks bad, it's true,' said Holmes. 'But the young man is **innocent**, I **believe**.'

'Innocent?' said Holder. 'Then why did he have the crown? And why did he say nothing?'

'His **silence** is very interesting,' said Holmes. 'An innocent man speaks a lot and tells you everything. A guilty man speaks a lot, but he is a liar. But to say nothing is most unusual. Did Arthur really go to your office, break off a corner of the crown, go to put it in a safe place, and then come back to the office with the **remainder** of the crown? I can't believe it!'

'But then what really happened last night?' asked Holder.

'Well, let's go to your house in Streatham now,' said

guilty doing something wrong

innocent doing nothing wrong

believe to think that something is true

silence when a person doesn't speak

remainder what is there when you take away part of something

Holmes. 'And perhaps we can find the answer to that question. Come along too, Watson.'

I was, of course, happy to go with them to investigate this strange case.

Holmes didn't speak in the carriage. He sat with his hat over his eyes. When we arrived in Streatham, he stood and looked up at Holder's house.

The banker's home was an old white building with a big front garden. On the left of the house, there was a small lane to some **stables**. On the right, there was a **path** to the kitchen door. Holmes looked carefully at the snowy front garden. After that he walked down the path to the back of the house, and then into the stable lane.

Holder and I soon got cold, so we went into the house. We waited in silence in the warm room. Suddenly, a young woman came in. She had dark hair and big brown eyes. But her face was deadly white, and the whites of her eyes were red.

'Uncle,' she said. 'Is Arthur going to be free soon? Please say "yes"!'

'No, Mary. He must stay in the hands of the police for now,' answered Holder.

'But he's innocent. I'm sure of it,' said Mary.

'Then why does he continue with his silence?'

'Perhaps he's angry because you called him a thief and didn't believe him,' said Mary.

Holder then looked over at me. 'Mary, there is a detective here to investigate the crime.'

'This man here?' asked Mary.

'No, this is his friend, Dr Watson. The detective is in the

stables a building where horses live

path a way across a garden where people can walk

21

stable lane.'

'The stable lane?' she asked, and she looked worried.

Just then, Holmes walked in. 'Good morning,' he said. 'Miss Mary Holder? My name is Sherlock Holmes. I'd like to ask you one or two questions.'

Holmes and Mary sat at a table. 'Did you hear any noises last night?' asked Holmes.

'No,' said Mary. 'Nothing at all.'

'And did you close all the windows?' asked Holmes.

'Yes, I did,' said Mary.

'Now, you have a maid, Lucy. Is that right?'

'Yes,' said Mary. 'And you need to know something about her. She heard us talk about the crown at dinner, I believe.'

'I see,' said Holmes. 'And did Lucy meet her admirer at the kitchen door last night?'

'Yes, when I went to lock the door, Lucy came in. I saw a man behind her in the dark. It was Francis Prosper, the **greengrocer**. When we buy things in his shop, he brings them up to the house, and he likes to meet Lucy.'

'Does he have a false leg?' asked Holmes.

Mary looked afraid. 'Yes. How did you know that?' she asked. Then she smiled. 'You're a very good detective, Mr Holmes.'

'Does he have a false leg?'

Holmes looked back at Mary, but there was no smile on his face.

'I need to see the downstairs windows,' said the detective. He went and looked carefully at the window in the hall nearest the stable lane.

'Well, well,' he said quietly. 'Now, Mr Holder, Watson – let's go upstairs to the office.'

In the office Holmes went to the desk. 'Which key did the thief open the desk with?' he asked.

'The key to the attic,' said Holder. 'You know, Arthur talked about it at dinner.'

'I remember,' said Holmes.

'And here is the famous Emerald Crown,' said Holder. He took it out of the box and put it on the table. We all stood in silence and looked at the beautiful emeralds.

'Now, Mr Holder,' said Holmes. 'I want you to break off a second corner of the crown here.'

'No!' said Holder.

'Well, watch me do it,' said Holmes. He quickly pulled the corner of the crown, but nothing happened. 'Do you see? I'm a big man, but I can't break it. And think about it, Mr Holder, when gold breaks, it makes a loud noise. Did you hear a loud noise last night?'

'No,' said Holder. 'No, I didn't.'

'Good. That's all then,' said Holmes.

'But where are the missing emeralds?' asked Holder. 'And what's going to happen to Arthur.'

'I can't say now,' said Holmes.

'But what really happened last night? Please tell me!'

'Come to my house tomorrow between nine and ten. Perhaps I can tell you then. Goodbye.'

activities

READING CHECK

Choose the right words to finish the sentences.

a Holder and Mary often . . .
1 ☐ play cards.
2 ☑ stay at home.
3 ☐ go out.

b Arthur is . . . Holmes believes.
1 ☐ guilty of the crime
2 ☐ innocent of the crime
3 ☐ sorry about the crime

c When Holmes arrives at Holder's house, he stays for a long time in the . . .
1 ☐ carriage.
2 ☐ stables.
3 ☐ garden and stable lane.

d Mary wants Arthur to . . .
1 ☐ be free soon.
2 ☐ stay with the police.
3 ☐ go and live in a different house.

e At the kitchen door last night, Lucy met . . .
1 ☐ Francis Prosper, the greengrocer.
2 ☐ the greengrocer's son.
3 ☐ a man with two false legs.

f When Holmes pulls at the Emerald Crown, he . . .
1 ☐ slowly breaks it.
2 ☐ can't break it.
3 ☐ quickly breaks it and makes a loud noise.

WORD WORK

1 Find six more words from the story round the crown.

2 Use the words from Activity 1 to complete the notes in Holmes's notebook on page 25.

24

a Who walked along the ....p̲a̲t̲h̲.... in the front garden last night?

b Why doesn't Arthur talk? Why does he continue with his ....?

c Arthur is not a really bad young man. He's .... , I'm sure.

d Where is the missing part of the crown?
And why did Arthur have the .... of it in his hands?

e Did somebody walk down the stable .... last night?

f Why did the .... come to the kitchen door last night? Is he .... of taking the crown?

GUESS WHAT

What happens in the next chapter? Tick two boxes.

a ☐ Holmes puts on a nice new coat. He goes out to meet Mary Holder.

b ☐ Holmes and Watson continue to investigate the crime.

c ☐ Holder goes to see Holmes again. He is very worried and unhappy.

d ☐ Holder gets a letter from his son. He is very happy about it.

e ☐ Holmes finds the missing corner of the Emerald Crown.

~~ Chapter FIVE ~~
'You are near the end of your trouble.'

olmes and I took a carriage back to Baker Street. He talked about the weather but, of course, I wanted to know more about the case. I asked him a number of questions: 'Is Arthur guilty, do you think?' 'Where are the missing emeralds?' But every time Holmes went back to the weather. So I stopped asking my questions, and looked out of the window.

It was three o'clock when we arrived at Baker Street. Holmes walked quickly into the house. 'I have a lot more work to do on this case,' he said. And with that, he ran upstairs to his room.

After some minutes, he came downstairs in an old coat, a black hat, and some dirty brown shoes. He looked in the hall mirror. 'What do you think, Watson?' he asked.

'Very good, Holmes,' I answered. 'You're the picture of a working man.'

'Thank you, Watson,' smiled Holmes. 'I'm sorry but you can't come with me this time. Well, see you later this

'What do you think, Watson?'

afternoon. Goodbye.' He pulled his hat down over his face, and went out into the street.

It was nearly six o'clock when Holmes came back. 'Hello, Watson,' he said happily. 'Can you take this?' He gave me an old black shoe.

'But what's it for?' I asked.

'I can't **explain** now,' he said. 'I'm going out again. To the West End this time. I'm going to be late home, I think, so don't wait for me.'

'And how's it all going?' I asked.

'All right. I went over to Streatham again this afternoon, but I didn't call at the house,' he said. 'But I mustn't sit here and talk. I must take off these old things. I need to be Sherlock Holmes once again.'

Holmes was very pleased with his work that day, I could see. He went upstairs, and five minutes later, the front door closed behind him. He was out on his detective work once again.

I sat and waited all evening for Holmes to come back. When it was midnight, I went up to bed. I wasn't surprised. Holmes was often out late. When he investigated a case, he was sometimes away for days and nights.

What time did he come in? I don't know, but he was there at breakfast. He had a coffee in one hand, and a big smile on his face.

'Good morning, Watson,' he said. 'Sorry to start breakfast without you. But Holder is coming here at nine. You remember that, surely.'

explain to talk to someone and make them understand something

'But it's after nine now,' I answered. 'And I heard someone at the front door a short time ago.'

Just then, the maid brought in our friend, Mr Holder. He walked slowly into the room. I pulled out a chair for him, and he fell into it. I was very surprised when I saw him. His hair was whiter than before, and his face looked very tired.

'Why is this happening to me?' he asked. 'Only two days ago I was a happy man. Now everything in my world looks black. This morning one more **terrible** thing happened in my house. My niece, Mary, left me.'

'Left you?' asked Holmes.

'Yes. She wasn't at breakfast this morning, and there was this letter for me on the hall table.'

Holder read the letter to us:

Dear Uncle,

You and Arthur are **in trouble** because of me. I can't stay any longer in your house. I must leave you and never come back. I am going to move far away from here, so please don't look for me.

Thank you for all the things you did for me.

Your loving Mary

'What is this letter all about?' asked Holder.

terrible very bad

in trouble with problems

'This is all for the best, I'm sure,' said Holmes. 'You know, Mr Holder, you are near the end of your trouble, I believe.'

'Do you know something about the emeralds, Mr Holmes?' asked Holder.

'Perhaps,' said Holmes. 'Is three thousand pounds a lot to get the emeralds back, do you think?'

'No,' said Holder. 'Three thousand is nothing!'

'Well, write me a **cheque** for three thousand pounds then,' said Holmes.

Holder wrote the cheque, and gave it to Holmes. The detective suddenly took out the missing corner of the crown from his pocket.

'You have it!' shouted Holder.

'Yes, I do. And now you need to do one more thing for somebody,' said Holmes.

'And what's that?' asked Holder.

'You need to say sorry to your son, Arthur,' said Holmes.

'Is he innocent then?' asked Holder.

'I told you this yesterday,' said Holmes, 'and I say it again today.'

'Are you sure of it now?' asked Holder.

'Yes, I am,' said Holmes.

'Then let's go and tell Arthur at once.'

'It's all right. He knows,' said Holmes. 'When I learned the **truth**, I went to talk to him. I told him my story, and he said, "You're right, Mr Holmes!"'

'Well, Holmes,' cried Holder. 'So what really happened on that terrible night? You must tell me now.'

'You have it!'

READING CHECK

Correct six more mistakes in this summary of Chapter 5.

three

Holmes and Watson go back to Baker Street at ~~nine~~ o'clock. Holmes puts on the clothes of

a rich man. Then he goes out. He comes home with an old black bag, and he gives it to

Watson. Holmes then goes out again, and he arrives home before midnight.

The next day, Holmes and Watson are having lunch when Holder comes to the house.

Holder shows them a letter from his son, Arthur.

Holmes asks Holder for a cheque, and Holder quickly writes a cheque for three hundred

pounds. Holmes then takes out the missing corner of the Emerald Crown.

WORD WORK

Use the letters in the hats to make words. Then write the sentences.

a I need to write you a **qchuee** because all my money is at home.

I need to write you a cheque because all my money is at home

b Don't go to see that new film – it's **rterbeli** !

....

c My friend is **ni ruobelt** because he was late for school this morning.

....

d Our teacher sometimes **xliasepn** new words to us in class.

....

e I don't believe her because she never tells the **ruhtt**

....

30

GUESS WHAT

What do we learn in the next chapter? Tick the boxes.

a Who are lovers?

1 ☐ Mary and Burnwell   **2** ☐ Mary and Francis Prosper   **3** ☐ Lucy and Arthur

b Who had a fight on the night of the crime?

1 ☐ Arthur and Francis Prosper   **2** ☐ Francis Prosper and Burnwell   **3** ☐ Arthur and Burnwell

c Who took the crown?

1 ☐ Lucy and Francis Prosper   **2** ☐ Mary and Burnwell   **3** ☐ Lucy and Burnwell

Chapter six

All in a day's work

'**M**r Holder, before I explain things,' said Holmes. 'I must tell you something. It's not going to be easy for me to say it, and it's not going to be easy for you to hear it. Your niece, Mary, and Sir George Burnwell are lovers. Yesterday she ran away with him.'

'My Mary?' said Holder. 'I don't believe you. It isn't true!'

'I'm sorry, but it is,' said Holmes. 'When Burnwell first visited your house, you didn't know much about him. But he is one of the worst men in England – a liar and a thief. He lost all his money years ago in the gambling clubs of London.

'Mary loved this handsome man. She met him every night at the window by the stable lane. Mary knew nothing of men, and she was soon under his terrible power.

'She met him every night at the window by the stable lane.'

'On the night of the crime,' continued Holmes, 'Mary met Burnwell by the window and told him about the Emerald Crown. Burnwell thought, "I can get a lot of money for this crown!" So he asked Mary, "Can you bring it to me later this evening?" And she said, "Yes."

'When you came downstairs, Mary stopped speaking to Burnwell and quickly closed the window. She then told you about Lucy meeting her admirer. That was the truth, of course, but it happened earlier.

'Arthur went to bed after his angry talk with you. He slept badly, and got up in the night when he heard a noise. He looked out of his door, and saw Mary go into your office. She came out with the crown, and took it downstairs. Arthur went after her, and saw more. Downstairs Mary gave the crown to somebody through the open stable lane window. After that, she went back to her room.

'Arthur loved Mary, and he didn't want people to know about her crime. But he needed to get the crown back, so he dressed quickly, and went downstairs. He jumped out of the window without any shoes on, and ran after a man in the stable lane. It was, of course, our friend Burnwell.

'Arthur pulled Burnwell down into the snow. Then he hit Burnwell above the eye. The men pulled at the crown between them. Suddenly something broke, and the crown was in Arthur's hands.

'He went back into the house, closed the window behind him, and ran upstairs to your office. The crown was **twisted,** he could see, and he wanted to put it right.

'And then Mr Holder, you came in,' said Holmes.

'Yes,' cried Holder unhappily. 'I saw Arthur pull wildly at

twisted when something has the wrong shape

the crown with his hands. Now I understand.'

'You then made Arthur angry. You called him a liar and a thief! And he couldn't explain. He didn't want you to know about Mary's crime.'

'And Mary fell down when she saw the crown,' said Holder. 'Now I understand that too. And Arthur asked, "Can I go out for five minutes?" That was because he wanted to look for the missing emeralds.'

Holder looked unhappy. 'Oh, Mr Holmes, I was very wrong about my son. But how did you learn all this?'

'Well,' said Holmes, 'the snow was a big help to me. Remember when I went out and looked at the garden at your house?'

'Yes,' said Holder.

'I could see much of the story of that terrible night in the snow,' he explained. 'When I walked up the path, I saw **footprints** near the kitchen door. They were the footprints of a young woman and a man with a false leg.'

'Ah yes, Lucy and Francis Prosper,' said Holder. 'And was he the man in the garden on the night when I came back home with the crown?'

'Yes, that was Prosper. He came to meet your new maid Lucy,' said Holmes. He then explained more about the case.

footprint the hole that someone's foot makes in soft ground when they walk

set a number of things that go together

There were two **sets** of footprints in the snow in the stable lane. The first set was of a man in big shoes. These footprints were next to the stable lane window, and the man waited there for a long time, I could see. The footprints then went down the lane to a tree.

The second set of footprints was of a man with no shoes. They came from the window out into the lane. They too went down to the tree. In the snow I could see the story of a fight between the two men. I found some **blood** there.

Then the first set of footprints went off down the lane. The second set of footprints came back to the window.

You remember when, in your house, I looked carefully at the window by the lane. I saw a footprint of the man with no shoes there, so he came back in through the window, I knew.

I started to understand the case better. The man with no shoes was Arthur. But I had two questions. Who was the man in the lane? And who brought the crown to this man? Well, it wasn't Arthur, so Mary or one of the maids was the guilty one.

blood this is red; You can see it when you cut your hand

I found some blood there.

Arthur's silence was important. He wanted to **protect** somebody. It wasn't Lucy or the younger maids – it was Mary, because he loved her.

But who helped Mary with the crime? Mary was a good young woman. But perhaps a lover had power over her and made her do this terrible thing. So who was her lover?

Only one or two visitors came to your house, you said. One of those was Burnwell. My friends told me about him some years ago – he had a bad name with women then, and he has a worse name with women now.

But was Burnwell really the thief? I wanted to be sure. So, after my visit to your house yesterday, I went home and put on an old working man's coat. I then visited Burnwell's house and spoke to his maid. She told me some interesting things, and I soon learnt about a **cut** over Burnwell's eye.

I also told the maid, 'I don't have any money, but I need some new shoes.' She felt sorry for me, and gave me some of Burnwell's old shoes.

I then went back to your house with one of the shoes. I was very pleased when it **fitted** the footprint in the snow.

After that, I came back to Baker Street, put on my usual coat, and went over to Burnwell's house again. I badly wanted the emeralds back. But I didn't want any scandal for the royal family – so no policemen, no open investigation.

I spoke to Burnwell at his house for some time. At first he said, 'I know nothing of the Emerald Crown.' But when I explained all about the crime, he became angry. He started to hit me, but I took out my **pistol** and put it to his head.

He then found a box, and opened it angrily. The missing emeralds were in it. 'Give me three thousands pounds for them,' he said. Of course, I didn't want to give the man any

protect to save someone or something from danger

cut a place where blood comes from your body after someone hits it

fit to be the right size

pistol a person can kill someone with this

money. But I also didn't want him to talk and make a scandal. So I wrote a cheque, took the box, and left. I got to bed at two o'clock in the morning. It was the end of a very long day's work.

'A day when you stopped a terrible scandal from happening!' said Holder. 'I can't find words to thank you,' and he stood up to go. 'Now I must find my son and say sorry for not believing him. Goodbye, Mr Holmes, Dr Watson.' And with that, he left.

I looked at Burnwell's old shoe on the table in front of me.

'You always find the answer in the end, Holmes,' I said.

'It's all in a day's work, Watson,' smiled Holmes.

I took out my pistol and put it to his head.

READING CHECK

1 Correct the mistakes in these sentences.

a Mary and Sir George Burnwell are ~~friends~~. *lovers*

b Burnwell is one of the best men in the country.

c Mary met Burnwell at the door by the stable lane.

d Arthur saw Mary go downstairs with the key.

e In the fight Arthur hit Burnwell above the mouth.

f Holmes found two sets of emeralds in the snow in the stable lane.

g Holmes visited Burnwell's house and spoke to his gardener.

h Holmes took out his knife and put it to Burnwell's head.

i Holder wants to say goodbye to his son.

WORD WORK

Use the words round the shoe to complete the sentences on page 39.

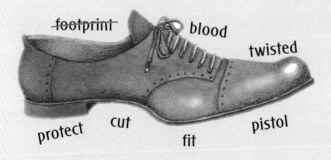

~~footprint~~   blood   twisted

protect   cut   fit   pistol

activities

GUESS WHAT

What happens after the end of the story? Tick the boxes.

		Yes	No
a	People hear about the case of the Emerald Crown. There's a big scandal.	☐	☐
b	Arthur begins to work at his father's bank.	☐	☐
c	Mary and Burnwell marry, but they are very unhappy.	☐	☐
d	Mary comes back to Holder's house and she marries Arthur.	☐	☐
e	Burnwell comes back to Holder's house and asks for more money.	☐	☐
f	Lucy the maid marries Francis Prosper and they are very happy.	☐	☐

39

PROJECT A *Crown jewels*

1 Read about the British Crown Jewels. Complete the table.

You can find the British Crown Jewels at the Tower of London. The Tower is a 900-year-old building near the River Thames in London. It's easy to get there by bus or underground train – the nearest underground station is Tower Hill.

You can visit the Crown Jewels from nine o'clock to half past five from Tuesday to Saturday and from ten o'clock on Sundays and Mondays.

You can see the Crown Jewels in the Jewel House. There are many different crowns, famous swords, and important jewels from the British royal family's past there. The most famous crown is the Imperial State Crown. It is gold, and it has 2,868 diamonds, 17 sapphires, and 11 emeralds in it!

What are the jewels called?	the British Crown Jewels
Where can you find them?	
How can you get there?	
When can you visit?	
Which building are the jewels in?	
What can you see there?	
Which is the most famous crown?	
Can you describe it?	

2 Use the notes in the table to write about the Austrian crown jewels.

What are the jewels called?	the Austrian crown jewels
Where can you find them?	the Hofburg Palace, Vienna
How can you get there?	by underground train: nearest station Stephansplatz
When can you visit?	from 10 o'clock to 6 o'clock Wednesday to Monday closed on Tuesdays
Which building are the jewels in?	the Treasury
What can you see there?	swords, jewels and crowns from the Austrian Imperial Family's past
Which is the most famous crown?	the Crown of Rudolph II
Can you describe it?	gold. It has a very big emerald, 8 diamonds, many rubies and sapphires, a large pearl from Panama and smaller pearls from Persia

3 Which different sets of famous jewels do you know about? Write about one of them.

Iranian Crown Jewels

Imperial Russian Crown Jewels

Hungarian Crown Jewels

PROJECT B *Sherlock Holmes's notebook*

1 Sherlock Holmes wrote notes about the night when a corner of the Emerald Crown went missing. Match them with one of the maps on page 43.

2 Read the notes again. Follow the footprints on the correct map. Find and correct two mistakes in the notes.

3 Sherlock Holmes also wrote notes about Mary. Where did she go on the night of the crime? Look at the correct map and complete the notes with the words in the box.

> *I found some interesting footprints — they are Francis Prosper's, I think.*
> *He went along the road, through the gate, down the path and round the tree. He then stopped at the kitchen door for a long time. Then he came back up the path, past the flower bed, across the lawn, through the gate and along the road again.*

across	*along*	*at*	*down*	*to*	*out*	*past*	*into*	*through*	*up*

On the night of the crime Mary went to bed. Later, she left her bedroom and went a) ...into... the office. She walked b) .... the room and opened the desk with the key. She came c) .... of the office with the Emerald Crown. Then she walked d) .... the stairs. She stopped e) .... the stable window and passed the crown to Burnwell f) .... the window. She then came back g) .... the stairs, and went h) .... the corridor, i) .... Holder's bedroom, and j) .... her bedroom.

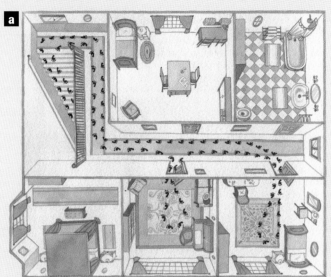

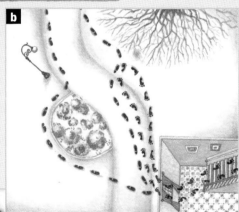

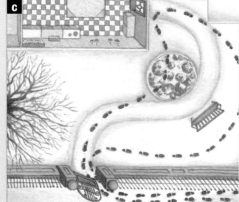

4 **Look at the map below. Which footprints are Arthur's? Which are Burnwell's? Complete the notes about Arthur's and Burnwell's movements on the night of the crime. Use Chapter Six of the story to help you.**

Arthur went down the stairs and then he ....

....

....

....

Burnwell came up the stable lane ....

....

....

....